Elbridge Jefferson Cutler

War Poems

Elbridge Jefferson Cutler

War Poems

ISBN/EAN: 9783744710664

Printed in Europe, USA, Canada, Australia, Japan

Cover: Foto ©Thomas Meinert / pixelio.de

More available books at **www.hansebooks.com**

To the Memory

OF

Brigadier-General CHARLES RUSSELL LOWELL,

Colonel POWELL TREMLETT WYMAN,

Lieutenant-Colonel WILDER DWIGHT,

AND

Major FITZHUGH BIRNEY.

CONTENTS.

REVEILLE.

THE drum's wild roll awakes the land ; the
    fife is calling shrill ;
Ten thousand starry banners blaze on town
    and bay and hill ;
The thunders of the rising war drown Labor's
    peaceful hum,
And heavy to the ground the first dark drops
    of battle come :
Thank God ! we are not buried yet, though
    long in trance we lay ; —
Thank God ! the fathers need not blush to
    own their sons to-day !

O, scarcely was there faith in God, nor any
trust in man,
While fast along the southern sky the blight-
ing shadow ran :
It veiled the stars one after one ; it hushed the
household song,
And stole from men the sacred sense that
parteth right and wrong.
Then a fierce, sudden flash across the ragged
blackness broke,
And with a voice that shook the land the
guns of Sumter spoke :
Wake, sons of heroes, wake ! The age of heroes dawns again ;
Truth takes in hand her ancient sword, and
calls her loyal men.
Lo ! brightly o'er the breaking day shines Freedom's holy star ;
Peace cannot cure the sickly time. All hail
the healer, War !

That voice the Empire City heard; 't was
    heard in Boston Bay ;
Then to the lumber-camps of Maine sped on
    its eager way :
Over the breezy prairie-lands, by bluff and lake
    it went,
To where the Mississippi shapes the plastic con-
    tinent ;
Then on, by cabin and by fort, by stony
    wastes and sands,
It rang exultant down the sea where the
    Golden City stands.
And wheresoe'er the summons came, there rose
    an angry din,
As when upon a rocky coast a stormy tide
    sets in.
Hurrah ! the long despair is past ; our fading
    hopes renew ;
The fog is lifting from the land, and lo the
    steadfast blue !

The old men bless the young men and
  praise their bearing high ;
The women in the doorways stand to wave
  them bravely by :
One threw her arms about her boy, and said,
  " Good by, my son,
God help thee do the valiant deeds thy father
  would have done ! "
One held up to a bearded man a little child
  to kiss,
And said, " I shall not be alone, for thy dear
  love and this."
And one, a lily in her hand, drooped at a sol-
  dier's side ; —
" Thy country weds thee first," she said.   " Be
  I thy second bride ! "

O mothers ! when you fold away the garments of your son, —
The shapely staff your weary years were fain
  to lean upon ;

O wives! when o'er the cradled child you bend
    at evening's fall,
And voices which the heart can hear across
    the distance call ;
O maids! when in the sleepless nights you ope
    the little case,
And look till you can look no more upon the
    proud young face ; —
Not only pray the Lord of life, who measures
    mortal breath,
To bring the absent back, unscathed, out of the
    fire of death ; —
But pray with that divine content which God's
    best favor draws,
That, whosoever lives or dies, He save His holy
    cause !

Sweet is the praise of harvest-home, of syl-
    van haunts and brooks,
Of red swords into ploughshares beat, of spears
    to pruning-hooks,

Of the long splendor of the Arts the fervid
    years disclose ;
But 'mid the victories of Peace, the heart a-
    straying goes
From field of glory unto field where, since the
    world began,
The hosts of good and ill have met, and men
    have died for man.
Our mortal bodies are but earth, and thrive
    on earthly bread ;
On generous hopes and noble faiths our sub-
    tler souls are fed :
Truth flashes from the clash of arms, as from
    the troubled sea
Sprang Venus in the immortal bloom of youth
    and deity !
So, sweeter than the song of Peace, the ring-
    ing battle-shout,
When Error's thistle-calyx bursts, Truth's pur-
    ples blossom out ;

And lovelier than the waving grain, the bat-
tle-flag unfurled

Amid the din of trump and drum to lead the
onward world!

Then mothers, sisters, daughters! spare the
tears you fain would shed:

Who seem to die in such a cause, you cannot
call them dead!

O, length of days is not a boon the brave
man prayeth for;

There are a thousand evils worse than death
or any war:

Oppression, with his iron strength fed on the
souls of men;

And License, with the hungry brood that ken-
nel in his den.

But Law, the form of Liberty! God's light is
on thy brow;

And Liberty, the soul of Law! God's very self
art thou.

Divine ideas! we write your names across our
    banner's fold;
For you the sluggard's brain is fire, for you
    the coward bold.
Fair ˍdaughter of the bleeding Past! Bright
    hope the Prophets saw!
God give us Law in Liberty, and Liberty in
    Law!

Hurrah! the drums are beating; the fife is
    calling shrill;
Ten thousand starry banners flame on town
    and bay and hill:
The thunders of the rising war hush Labor's
    drowsy hum;
Thank God that we have lived to see the saf-
    fron morning come! —
The morning of the battle-call, to every sol-
    dier dear : —
O joy! the cry is "Forward!" O joy! the foe
    is near!

For all the crafty men of peace have failed to
    purge the land :
Hurrah! the ranks of battle close ; God takes
    his cause in hand !

IO TRIUMPHE!

NOW let us raise a song of praise, like
Miriam's song of old, —
A song of praise to God the Lord, for bless-
ings manifold!
He lifteth up, He casteth down; He bindeth,
setteth free;
He sendeth grace to bear defeat; He giveth
victory!

O, hear ye how from Somerset the voice of
triumph calls!
Hear how the echoes take it up on Henry's
conquered walls!

And wilder yet the thrilling cry : Fort Donelson is ours!

Like chaff before the roaring North fly fast
the Rebel powers ;

New Orleans sees her doom afar, and lifts a
palsied arm,

And haughty Richmond's drunken streets are
sobered with alarm ;

Up Carolina's frantic shore the tide rolls black
and dire :

The thunder's voice is in its heart, its crest
avenging fire !

On inland slopes and by the sea are wreck
and flying foe ;

And fresh in that unwonted air the flowers of
freedom blow !

Then honor, under God, to those, the noble
men who plan,

And unto those of fiery mould, who flame in
battle's van !

For, O, the land is safe, is safe; it rallies from
the shock!

Ring round, ring round, ye merry bells, till
every steeple rock!

Let trumpets blow and mad drums beat! let
maidens scatter flowers!

The sun bursts through the battle-smoke!
Hurrah! the day is ours!

FEB. 18, 1862.

DEFEAT.

THE God of Israel is our God, who set
    his people free,
Through fire and storm and desert heats and
    slimy depths of sea.
So, while the thunder's arrow smites and angry
    lightnings play,
He leads us to the promised land, by this His
    chosen way.

Let not a wailing cry be heard, no tear of
    sorrow fall ;
In silence follow to the grave the dead beneath
    yon pall !

Not yet plant we the votive stone, nor mock-
ery of bloom ;
But let us swear a solemn oath beside the
open tomb : —

In His dread name whose throne is law, in
theirs who sleep below,
Into the fiery gulf of war, our lives, our hopes
we throw :
We draw the sword our fathers blessed, and
cast the sheath away,
To conquer back these dead men's fame, or lie
as cold as they !

When we have won the right to weep, the
right to praise the brave,
Then be the lofty marble brought to mark the
soldier's grave :

Around it let the ivy creep with roses side by
    side ;
And all in shining gold be writ his name and
    how he died !

But now shed not the useless tear, lift not the
    voice of woe !
The earth is red with kindrèd blood, — before
    us is the foe !
The cannon's roar, the sword's keen flash, the
    unrelenting eye,
These be our wail at sore defeat, these be our
    proud reply !

JULY 4, 1862.

THE SOLDIERS' RALLY.

O RALLY round the banner, boys, now
    Freedom's chosen sign!
See where amid the clouds of war its new-
    born glories shine!
The despot's doom, the slave's dear hope, we
    bear it on the foe!
God's voice rings down the brightening path!
    Say, brothers, will ye go?

"My father fought at Donelson; he hailed
    at·dawn of day
That flag full-blown upon the walls, and proud-
    ly passed away."

"My brother fell on Newbern's shore; he
    bared his radiant head,
And shouted, 'On! the day is won!' leaped
    forward, and was dead."
"My chosen friend. of all the world hears not
    the bugle-call;
A bullet pierced his loyal heart by Rich-
    mond's fatal wall."
But seize the hallowed swords they dropped,
    with blood yet moist and red!
Fill up the thinned, immortal ranks, and fol-
    low where they led!
For Right is might, and Truth is God, and
    He upholds our cause,
The grand old cause our fathers loved, —
    Freedom and Equal Laws!

"My mother's hair is thin and white; she
    looked me in the face;
She clasped me to her heart, and said, 'Go,
    take thy brother's place!'"

"My sister kissed her sweet farewell; her
 maiden cheeks were wet;
Around my neck her arms she threw; I feel
 the pressure yet."
"My wife sits by the cradle's side and keeps
 our little home,
Or asks the baby on her knee, 'When will
 thy father come?'"
The shrieking shell may burst in fire, the
 whizzing bullet fly;
The heavens and earth may mingle grief, the
 gallant soldier die:
While Treason lifts its scornful crest, no
 peace! for peace is war;
The land that is not worth our death is not
 worth living for!

Then' rally round the banner, boys! Its
 triumph draweth nigh!
See where above the clouds of war its seam-
 less glories fly!

Peace, hovering o'er the bristling van, waves
    palm and laurel fair ;
And Victory binds the rescued stars in Free-
    dom's golden hair !

JAN. 1, 1863.

THE VOLUNTEER.

"AT dawn," he said, "I bid them all farewell,
     To go where bugles call and rifles gleam."
And with the restless thought asleep he fell,
     And wandered into dream.

A great hot plain from sea to mountain
          spread ;
     Through it a level river slowly drawn :
He moved with a vast crowd, and at its head
     Streamed banners like the dawn.

There came a blinding flash, a deafening roar,
     And dissonant cries of triumph and dismay ;

Blood trickled down the river's reedy shore,
   And with the dead he lay.

The morn broke in upon his solemn dream ;
  And still with steady pulse and deepening
     eye,
" Where bugles call," he said, "and rifles
     gleam,
   I follow, though I die !"

CAVALRY SONG.

THE squadron is forming, the war-bugles
play !
To saddle, brave comrades, stout hearts for a
fray !
Our captain is mounted, — strike spurs, and
away !

No breeze shakes the blossoms or tosses the
grain ;
But the wind of our speed floats the galloper's
mane,
As he feels the bold rider's firm hand on the
rein.

Lo, dim in the starlight their white tents ap-
    pear!
Ride softly! ride slowly! the onset is near!
More slowly! more softly! the sentry may hear!

Now fall on the foe like a tempest of flame!
Strike down the false banner whose triumph
    were shame!
Strike, strike for the true flag, for freedom and
    fame!

The bugles recall us; the carnage is done:
All red with our valor, we welcome the sun.
Hurrah! sheathe your swords! we have won!
    we have won!

LULLABY.

NOW the twilight shadows flit;
  Now the evening lamp is lit:
    Sleep, baby, sleep!
Little head on mother's arm,
She will keep him safe from harm, —
Keep him safe and fold him warm!
    Sleep, baby, sleep!

Baby's father, far away,
Thinks of him at shut of day:
    Sleep, baby, sleep!
He must guard the sleeping camp,

Hearkening, in the cold and damp,
For the foeman's stealthy tramp.
 Sleep, baby, sleep!

He can hear the lullaby,
He can see the laughing eye:
 Sleep, baby, sleep!
And he knows, though we are dumb,
How we long to have him come
Back to baby, mother, home.
 Sleep, baby, sleep!

Baby's eyes are closing up;
Let their little curtains drop!
 Sleep, baby, sleep!
Softly on his father's bed
Mother lays her darling's head;
There until the night be fled,
 Sleep, baby, sleep!

God, who dry'st the widow's tears,
God, who calm'st the orphan's fears,
Guard baby's sleep!
Shield the father in the fray;
Help the mother wait and pray;
Keep us all by night and day!
Sleep, baby sleep!

A COLONEL'S LAST WORDS.

Some random thoughts
Which you shall put in letters to my friends.
Say:—

LIFE is sweet for the mere living's sake,
    And sweet to me for many things to do,—
Hopes unfulfilled, and loves unrecompensed,—
A mother's, and a brother's, and a wife's,
And this strange love of grown-up men. For
        all
My soldiers love me, their plain way; each
        knows
My thought is of him, how he may be strong,
And, by war's discipline, a better man.

I hold that he, the lawless, violent,
When once he puts his country's armor on,
Making his breast her bulwark, by that grace,
Compensates all a life of private crime.

Yes, life is sweet, and yet death is not bitter ;
For some serve in their lives, some in their
      deaths,
And the great Fate, that meteth each to each,
Knows neither passion nor remorse. The lot
Is equal, and the service, and the gain.

In peace, I took the temper of the time, —
Most pliable and sluggish of recoil ;
But the war-fires have seasoned me to use,
Toughened the tender fibres of my growth,
That I might drive the arrow straight to the
      targe.
Let war be war, the fiercer, better war !
Let the torch burn and the blue bullet slay !

So shall the peace to come be peace indeed.
For not a drop of blood is shed in vain,
Not theirs nor ours: ours witnesses the right ;
Theirs is as red, and expiates the wrong.

Then tell the mother she must spare her
    son,
And tell the wife to let her husband go !
The Past and Future, as on mountain-tops,
O'erlook the field and cheer his valor on.
In their impartial eyes there is no rank
Save what his strain of merit wins a man ;
No honor save in loyalty to Truth.

Great purposes are absolute of means :
Not one can choose his attitude of doing,
When Xanthos and Achilles wage the war
As old as God, irreconcilable,
'Twixt the old form outlingering its age, ·
And the new form impatient to succeed.

All day the battle raged, and the red land
And all the sea as far as Tenedos
Were horrible with corpses, till Hephaistos
Blasted the evil river to its source.

JANUARY, 1865.

A DIRGE.

κεῖσυ μέγας μεγαλωστί, λελασμένος ἱπποσυνάων.
ἡμεῖς δὲ πρύπαν ἦμαρ ἐμαρνάμεθ'.

MOURN for the young!
  Mourn for the brave!
He sleeps beneath the sod,
With all the stars of God
To watch his grave.
He gave himself for us
In battle glorious, —
And shall he go unsung?

Mourn for the young!
Mourn for the brave!

About his gallant head
Did battle-banners wave ;
About his dying bed
The bullet sung ;
The cannon's thunder rung
The triumph in his ear.
The spirit is with God ;
The body with the clod ;
But memory with us here.

Vanished like a vanished flame, —
That comprehensive wit,
That nobleness of aim,
And force to compass it.
Glory claims him hers, and we
Must lay him down.
There is none left like thee,
King jewel of our crown !
But when a hero dies,
Thank God ! the cause

Of country, freedom, laws,
Lives by the sacrifice!

Mourn for the young!
Mourn for the brave!
The slow vine creeps around
The soldier's grave.
Long be votive garlands flung
Upon the sacred mound!
And when a hundred years
Lose record of our tears,
Still will the voice of fame
Exult to name his name;
And every spring the clover and the sorrel
Make haste to bloom for crown and laurel!

THE REGIMENT'S RETURN.

I.

H E is coming, he is coming, my true love
comes home to-day!
All the city throngs to meet him, as he lingers
by the way.
He is coming from the battle with his knap-
sack and his gun, —
He, a hundred times my darling, for the dan-
gers he hath run!

Twice they said that he was dead, but I
would not believe the lie;

While my faithful heart kept loving him, I knew
    he could not die.

All in white will I array me, with a rose-bud
    in my hair,

And his ring upon my finger,—he shall see it
    shining there:

He will kiss me, he will kiss me, with the kiss
    of long ago;

He will fold his arms around me close, and I
    shall cry, I know.

O, the years that I have waited, rather lives
    they seemed to be,

For the dawning of the happy day that brings
    him back to me!

But the worthy cause has triumphed, O joy!
    the war is over!

He is coming, he is coming, my gallant sol-
    dier-lover!

II.

MEN are shouting all around me, women weep
and laugh for joy,
Wives behold again their husbands, and the
mother clasps her boy ;
All the city throbs with passion ; 't is a day of
jubilee :
But the happiness of thousands brings not happiness to me.

I remember, I remember, when the soldiers
went away,
There was one among the noblest who is not
returned to-day.
O, I loved him, how I loved him ! and I never
can forget
That he kissed me as we parted, for the kiss
is burning yet !

'T is his picture in my bosom, where his head
    will never lie ;
'T is his ring upon my finger, — I will wear
    it till I die.
O, his comrades say that, dying, he looked up
    and breathed my name :
They have come to those that loved them, but
    my darling never came.
O, they say he died a hero, — but I knew how
    that would be ;
And they say the cause has triumphed — Will
    that bring him back to me ?

SONNET.

THE flag is folded ; for the battle's din,
  The cry of trumpet and the blaze of gun,
The thunderous rush of squadrons closing in,
  The stifled groan, the triumph-shout, are
    done.

And Peace is come, with passionless, mild
    eyes, —
A mother's eyes, a mother's tenderness ;
Calmed by her touch the weary nation lies,
  And feels her dewy breath upon his face.

But Time cannot avail, with all his years,
  Some chasms in our riven hearts to fill,
Whence misty memories rise to break in tears,
  And ghosts of buried hopes that haunt us
    still,

Yet bring a kind of joy, — the solemn trust
That form is more than unsubstantial dust.

SONNET.

IF generous parentage or breeding high,
　Or that fine strain where love and wit, at
　　　one,
　Put sisterly each other's jewels on,
Or flawless truth, or spotless purity,

Or beauty were an armor against Fate :
　Then thou, bright blended grace of man and
　　　boy,
　Sweet memory ! wouldst walk, a present joy,
With us, the sunny slope of life, elate !

Dear, blood-bought land, how precious for the
    cost !
Fair triumph, perfected by private pain !
    Bright manhood tried and proved beyond
      compare !

War wins an awful glory from that lost
    Nobility, which was not young in vain ;
      But Peace twines cypress in her flaxen
      hair.

RETREAT.

THE war was done, its harvest reaped, and
home the reapers came,
With garments worn and banners torn, but ri-
fles bright as flame.
Southward your valor swept, a hurricane of
steel and lead,
Amid the crash of blazing roofs the cannon's
cry of dread ;
Northward your laurelled legions bent, and
Fame before them ran,
And Victory on their standard shone, and
Freedom led the van.

What was the wondrous triumph, — what the
    priceless harvest reaped,
That cities put on flowers and fire, and happy
    women wept?
·O, write it on your proud façade, on arch and
    column stone
That once Right triumphed over Wrong, that
    Justice hath her own;
That science is the lord of force, by Nature's
    onward plan;
That ye had grace to do your work, so God
    did His for man!

Though loud and dark on heaven's rim, the
    tempest mutter still,
Fear not; for what is fear? The shadow of
    a feeble will.
Ye who have swept the old away, can ye not
    build the new?
O brothers who have bled for Truth, can ye
    not still be true?

Ye will not shrink, her chosen men, — she summons each by name ;
Before you burns your children's hope, behind,
   your fathers' fame !
So swear again in word and deed to keep the
   faith ye swore, —
By fire and sword, if that must be; but Freedom evermore !

TRANSLATIONS.

ANDROMACHE.

(Iliad, XXII., XXIV.)

NOW in the inmost chamber of the house,
Andromache sat weaving at the loom
An intricate purple web, distinct with flowers.
Her fair-haired household she had bid prepare
The steaming bath against her lord's return
From battle ; knowing not that Hector lay,
Slain by Achilles, on the dusty field.
But when she heard the wailment at the tower,
She shuddered, and the flashing shuttle dropped,
And with great heart-beats hurried to the wall ;
And saw, before the city, the fleet steeds

Dragging him towards the ships ; whereat she
    swooned.

Then from her head the beauteous garland fell,
The net, the fillet, and the shining veil
That golden Aphrodite gave, what time
Bright-plumèd Hector came with marriage
    gifts,
And led her from Eëtion's palace home.
And in their arms her sisters tended her
Who seemed as dead. But when she woke
    again,
And her sad soul returned upon her heart,
Sobbing she said among the Trojan dames : —

Alas ! O Hector ! a like evil fate
Was spun for me and thee, — thee here in
    Troy
In Priam's palace reared, me, hapless child,
By woody Plakos born. Thou passest down
The sad abysses of the underworld,

And leavest widowed me in desolate grief
To keep thy dwelling, with the boy, so young, —
Thy child and mine. Nor ever, Hector, wilt
Thou have a father's care of him, — for thou
Art dead, art dead, — nor he, a son's, of thee.
O, Hector, thou hast perished in thy youth,
Leaving the sorrowing city in dismay,
Leaving thy parents grief unutterable,
But chiefly grief to me ; for from thy bed
Thou didst not stretch thy dying hand to me,
Nor spakest words of counsel in my ear,
Which I might cherish, weeping night and
    day.

IPHIGENEIA.

(Lucretius, I. 88 – 101.)

NOW when the fillet bound her virgin hair,
 And equal fell on either cheek ; and
  when
She saw before the altar her sad sire,
Near him the priests concealing the sharp knife,
And all the people looking on in tears, —
Then dumb with fear she knelt ; but nought
  availed
The piteous maiden, in her time of need,
To be a princess, daughter of the King.
For she, uplifted in the hands of men,
Borne trembling to the altar, at the hour

Appointed for the bridal, yet no bride
With Hymeneal pomp, sinless, sinfully
Was slain, — a father's hapless victim, — that
Fair winds might blow the ships to prosperous
    war.

Cambridge : Printed by Welch, Bigelow, & Co.